Photographed
and edited
by

Pál Kolozs Huber

BUDAPEST

Contents

HISTORY OF BUDAPEST

Due to the favourable location of the city, in the natural and geographic centre of the Carpathian basin, at the meeting point of the mountains and plains divided by the Danube, people have lived here for thousands of years. Prehistoric man dwelt in the limestone caves of the Buda mountains. Finds from the early Bronze Age have attested that the place was inhabited around 2000 B.C. In the 5th and 4th centuries B.C., the Celts settled down in the area, founding a city renowned for its advanced industry and prosperous commerce.

In the early 1st century A.D., the Transdanubia region was named Pannonia by the conquering Romans. Aquincum, the most important city located at the heart of the province was built at the Óbuda (Old Buda) district of present-day Budapest. About 10,000 troops were stationed at a time at this legionary camp. These troops protected the stone houses, baths and the amphitheatre of the civilian population. The remains of Aquincum are now a museum. Huns arriving from the east populated the city after repeated raids had undermined Roman rule during the 5th century. Ancient Buda, the headquarters of Hun chieftain Attila, was probably located north of the ruins of the city deserted by the Romanized population. Legend has it that the city was named after Buda, Attila's elder brother. Following the collapse of Attila's empire, various ethnic groups arrived in the area in successive waves before the Avars established their state.

The conquering Magyars arrived in several waves to finally take hold of the entire Carpathian basin. The final wave of their tribes arrived in 896, led by Prince Árpád. The state of Hungary was founded by King St. Stephen (István) in 1000 A.D. The following centuries saw a steady development of the town.

Crossing a frozen Danube, invading Mongol troops burnt down the neighbouring cities of Pest and Buda in 1241. After their withdrawal, worried of further invasions, King Béla IV had the first royal stronghold built on top of the Castle Hill of Buda. Around the castle, Buda was fast developing into a medieval city of burghers with a national market-place. The city lived its brightest periods under the rule of Sigismund (Zsigmond, 1387-1437) and Matthias (Mátyás, 1458-1490). Under their rule, new courtyards and substantial buildings were added to the existing palace. Under Matthias' rule, Buda became the official capital, with its Renaissance palace famed all over Europe as a cultural centre, while Pest grew into a major commercial city.

In 1541, both cities were captured by the Turks who settled for Buda as their headquarters for the about 150 years of their occupation. Baths, bazaars and mosques were erected by settling Turkish tradesmen. With their highly ornamented, characteristic communal buildings built over springs of medicinal waters, the Turks introduced a bath culture that has survived to this day. In all other respects, however, the Turks neglected the city, whose buildings and artistic heritage fell

The Monument. The group of figures, the work of Zsigmond Kisfaludi Stróbl, was first erected in 1947 to commemorate the liberation of Budapest form Nazi rule.

BUDA CASTLE

The building of the Royal Castle was begun on the Castle Hill by King Béla IV in 1242, following the havoc wrought by the Mongol invasion. Apart from the natural beauty of the place, the central location and the strategic importance of the hill made it an ideal site for a city. In the 1360s Louis I set up his court and had his palace built here. The palace chapel had probably been built by that time. After that, it gradually became the permanent royal residence. Major constructions were resumed under Sigismund's rule. King Matthias employed Italian Renaissance masters for the constructions.

The Turkish sieges and finally the 1686 reoccupation destroyed the larger part of the castle, which remained in that condition until reconstruction began during the Baroque period. Maria Theresa restored and enlarged the Palace between 1748 and 1770, before it took its present-day shape under Emperor Franz Josef I in the following century. Miklós Ybl and Alajos Hauszmann were commissioned with the enlargement of the Baroque Palace respectively in 1881 and 1891. While they retained the existing contours of the building complex, they also added a genuine dome. During the fights of WWII, the castle was completely burnt out, the roofs fell down and the furniture was destroyed.

Several parts of the medieval palace and the royal city have been unearthed during the reconstruction, which began in 1946. Since then, the Budapest History Museum, the Hungarian National Gallery and the National Széchenyi Library have been relocated into the Castle. In 1988, UNESCO registered the Castle and its surroundings as a World Heritage site.

Funicular Railway with the 0 milepost. *Clinging to Castle Hill, the Funicular Railway was designed by Ödön Széchenyi in 1870. The world's second cable railway, it was equipped with the latest technology of the time. It climbs up a 48-degree slope, covering 95 metres.*

The coat-of-arms with cherubs. *The restored mosaic coat-of-arms of Hungary from 1880. The device translates: My trust in ancestral virtue.*

Sándor Palace. The Palace, designed by J. Aman and constructed from 1803 to 1806, now houses the Presidential Office.

Horse-herder statue. Modelled by sculptor György Vastagh on a Hortobágy horse-herder in 1899, the statue preserves the memory of the one-time royal riding-hall.

Turul. The mythical eagle spreads its wings above the Habsburg Stairway, built for the Millennium.

Gothic Castle Chapel. Built as a detached chapel in the 15th century, it was later incorporated into the Palace.

Lion Gate and Lion Courtyard. A gate guarded by four lions (sculpted by János Fadrusz) leads to the SW courtyard. This wing of the Palace is the home of the national library collection.

View of the Church of the Virgin Mary from the Schulek stairway. *Viewed from the east, the architectural genius of Frigyes Schulek achieved a harmonic unity between the church and the Fisherman's Bastion.*

Figures of the conquering chiefs *Under the southern arch of the grand staircase.*

MATTHIAS CHURCH

The Church of the Virgin Mary was consecrated in veneration of the Holy Virgin. It was erected during the 13th to the 15th centuries in Gothic style, over the remains of the parish church of the Germanic population that had settled in the Castle district during the 13th century. It was massively reconstructed during the reign of Louis I and Matthias. The latter built the higher tower and the royal oratory. Matthias Church, the name most commonly used today, originates from the time the building was constructed with generous financing by the king. The black raven, holding a ring in its beak, an important symbol of the king's coat-of-arms, appears on southern church-tower. Converted into a mosque during the Turkish period, its walls were whitewashed and the windows bricked up. The heavily damaged building was restored in Neo-Gothic style between 1874 and 1896 to designs by Frigyes Schulek.

The statue of the Madonna in the Loretto Chapel. The statue, made in 1515, appeared unexpectedly behind a collapsed wall when the powder-magazine was blown up in the siege of Buda in 1686. For the Turks, it was an omen of their imminent defeat.

The most striking detail of the church is the 72-metre high Matthias tower in the south. The northern Bale tower is covered with glazed tiles. The main western façade faces the Szentháromság (Holy Trinity) Square. The pyrogranite relief in the ridge of the main gate depicts the Madonna with the child. The large Gothic rosette is a faithful reconstruction of the rose-window bricked up during the Baroque period. The Maria Gate on the south was erected around 1370. The upper part of the finest gate has a relief showing Maria's death.

The internal ornamentation was designed by Frigyes Schulek, while the paintings and the stained glass decoration are the works of Bertalan Székely and Károly Lotz. The high altar depicts the Virgin Mary rise into heaven in a wreath of light.

In addition to its ecclesiastic functions, the church has always been a venue for luxurious secular ceremonies. It was the venue of the mass of Matthias' election to king and both his marriages. The last two kings, Franz Joseph I and Charles IV were crowned here in 1867 and 1916, respectively. The flags from the last coronation continue to embellish the walls.

Due to its excellent organ and perfect acoustics, major concerts are still held at the church. Outstanding first performances have included Liszt's Coronation Mass (1867) Kodály's Buda Castle Te Deum (1936). The church also houses a collection of ecclesiastic art.

The triple-nave church interior is illuminated from the south by three large stained-glass Gothic windows. The sanctuary in the northern side-aisle is dedicated to Ladislaus I of Hungary. Opening from the side-aisle, the Holy Trinity Chapel houses the sarcophagus of King Béla III and his wife as well as the Gothic winged wooden altarpiece of Saint Emeric's Chapel.

View from the steeple of the Matthias Church, commanding a majestic vista over the city.

Traceried stained-glass window from the southern front of the church. The works of Károly Lotz and Bertalan Székely, the three glass windows depict scenes from the lives of St. Margaret, St. Elisabeth of Hungary and the Virgin Mary. The window in the picture shows St. Margaret.

The roof of the Matthias Church. The colourful glazed tiles were produced at the famous Zsolnay factory of Pécs.

FISHERMAN'S BASTION

Based on a section of the medieval wall and designed by Frigyes Schulek, the bastion system at the eastern side of the Castle Hill was erected between 1895 and 1902. In the Middle Ages, the fish market was here and this part of the wall was defended by the Fishermen's Guild, which explains the origin of the name. The stairs, turrets and terraces were built in a blend of Neo-Romanesque, Neo-Gothic and Romantic styles. White limestone was used for the construction of the five circular, crested turrets and the main tower at the northernmost point. The turrets are connected by a stone breastwork and galleries over arcaded passages, reminiscent of medieval cloisters. The crypt of the 15th-century St. Michael cemetery chapel was unearthed under the Bastion. Designed for decorative rather than defensive purposes, the scenic bastion system provides a worthy frame for the buildings of the Castle and the Matthias Church. Its terraces command a magnificent view of the Pilis mountains toward the Danube Bend, the Margaret Island, the Danube bridges, Gellért Hill and the Pest side. The row of bastions, illuminated at night, offers a scenic view from the Pest riverfront.

King St. Stephen. *The large bronze statue was completed by Alajos Stróbl in 1906.*

The main tower of the Fisherman's Bastion. *The foiled, multi-storey tower was built over the remains of a former bastion. The stairways are decorated with the stone statues of chieftains Álmos and Elöd.*

Equestrian statue of King St. Stephen. *The marble reliefs on the Neo-Romanesque limestone plinth designed by Frigyes Schulek depict some famous scenes of the reign of the Apostolic king. The roofed Jesuit Staircase leads down from Castle Hill.*

Hess András Square with the Miklós Tower. The Hilton Hotel was built on the ruins of historic buildings north of Matthias Church. The Dominican St. Nicholas monastery was erected in the late 1770's. A 1930 replica of the relief showing King Matthias on his throne was placed on the wall of its incomplete Miklós Tower facing the square. Displaying the coats-of-arms of the subdued territories, it still carries the memory of the great king's empire.

Fortuna Street. This street connects Matthias Church with the Bécsi kapu Square. The country's first printing press operated in one of its medieval houses (1473).

14-16 Tárnok Street. *The upstairs sections, propped up by late 14th-century supports, were built during the 15th century. The geometric wall painting is a fine example of the faded glory of the streets of Buda.*

Szentháromság (Holy Trinity) Square. The Holy Trinity monument at the centre of the large square was erected out of gratitude in 1713, following the destruction caused by the Black Death. Depicted among the saints on the walls is St. Roch, patron saint of the invalid and of nursing. The square is a station for horse-drawn carriages taking tourists on a sightseeing tour of the Castle.

The Church of Maria Magdalena. *The ruins and Gothic window of the church are located on Kapisztrán Square.*

The Hungarian National Archives. *The Neo-Romanesque mansion is found on Bécsi kapu*

Military History Institute and Museum. *Museum entrance on Kapisztrán Square.*

View of the Castle *from the tower of Matthias Church.*

45-47 Úri Street. *A dwelling-house built in Neoclassical and Baroque styles.*

28 Úri Street. *The atmospheric inner courtyards are well-kept secrets of the Castle district.*

31 Úri Street. *Survives as the only authentic medieval three-storey building in the Castle district.*

Equestrian statue of András Hadik, *Maria Theresa's legendary cavalry general. Indeed, he hardly missed a battlefield in Europe.*

Pharmacy Museum. 18 Tárnok Street. *The statuette in the niche at the front is a Madonna by Margit Kovács.*

58 Úri Street. *Built on medieval foundations, the building was later converted in Neo-Baroque style.*

16 Táncsics Mihály Street. *This house was built over medieval ruins in the 18th century. A mural decorates its present-day Baroque façade.*

HOUSES OF PARLIAMENT

'As far as the new Parliament building is concerned, I had no intention to create a new style. One must take absolute care not to incorporate ephemeral details in such a monumental building, to be seen by centuries to come. Instead, I have endeavoured to blend into this splendid medieval style a kind of national and individual spirit in a restrained and careful manner, as a true artist should. To that end, I have used motifs of the Hungarian flora, the stylized plant forms of our meadows, forests and plains', wrote Imre Steindl, commissioned with the job of designing the Parliament building, in 1880.

Ornamented stairway. *Károly Lotz painted the frescoes on the ceiling of this glorious marble-walled hall decorated with statues, monumental columns and Baroque paintings that lend it a three-dimensional effect. The frescoes depict an apotheosis of legislation and the state of Hungary. The bust of architect Imre Steindl has been located in a niche on the landing. The stained-glass windows are the works of Miksa Róth.*

Vaulted hall. *The star-vaulted dome, resting on 16 posts, is 27 metres high. The posts carry the statues of Hungarian kings. The hall makes a worthy setting for the Holy Crown and the royal insignia.*

The House of Parliament, the symbol of the capital, the best-known and most impressive building in Hungary, is also one of the largest. Designed by Imre Steindl, it was constructed from 1885 to 1904. The first Parliamentary session was held in it on June 8th 1896.

The building's scale and proportions are enthralling: 268 by 118 metres, the dome rises 96 metres high over a surface of 17,745 square metres. This Eclectic palace is a mix of Neo-Gothic elements in its façade and elsewhere, whereas its ground-plan carries Baroque elements of composition. 365 slender turrets, the number of days in a year, give the building an ethereal grace. The Parliament building is decorated by 233 statues, 88 of which have been positioned on the exterior surfaces. The building has 27 gates, 10 courtyards, 29 stairways and 691 rooms. The total length of the stairs runs approximately 20 km.

Béla Markup's bronze lions sit guard of honour on both sides of the main entrance on Kossuth Lajos Square. The waterfront façade is decorated with statues of the seven conquering chiefs and the kings of Hungary, while generals and Transylvanian princes embellish the frontispiece overlooking the square. The unique ventilation system of the building maintains an even temperature of 20 °C throughout the year.

The Lounge. The hall, illuminated through glass windows, is ornamented by Zsolnay pyrogranite statutes, which symbolise industry, commerce, agriculture and sciences. The frescoes on the ceiling depict scenes from the Hun-Magyar folklore.

External view of the vaulted hall.

The Holy Crown is Hungary's national relic, the symbol of the Hungarian state. Having survived tempestuous centuries, it is one of the oldest initiatory crowns in Europe. Its pure gold is decorated with masterful enamel work, valuable jewels and genuine pearls. Under the cross, the Heavenly Father is shown sitting on his throne, with the figures of the apostles on the plates below. Depicted in the centre of the rim is Christ sitting enthroned, accompanied by the archangels Gabriel and Michael and the saints. The Holy Crown and the royal insignia were deposited with due solemnity in the vaulted hall of the house of legislation on January 1st 2000.

The Parliament from Kossuth Square.

Given that the old Hungarian Parliament was bicameral, the building contains two large, symmetric halls originally designed to accommodate the lower and the upper chambers. Today, the southern hall is used as the session-floor of Parliament, while conferences and international meetings are held in the northern chamber. In the two identical horse-shoe shaped chambers, the rows of the MPs' seats are laid out in a semicircle, with seats at the sides for visitors.

Details of the Parliament building

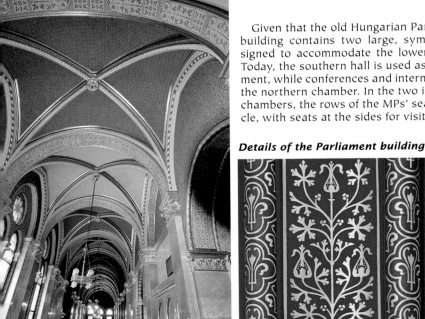

The Speaker's Platform. *The coats-of-arms of Hungarian dynasties are lined up next to the coat-of-arms of Hungary.*

The Chamber of Congress. *This chamber is decorated with a splendid wainscoted ceiling and marble lofts. Historical paintings have been positioned on both sides of the platform: the proclamation of the Golden Bull in 1222 and a scene in which the Hungarian estates offer their life and blood to Maria Theresa at the Parliament in Pozsony.*

Statue of Imre Nagy. *A small bridge serves as pedestal to the statue of the executed premier of the 1956 revolution, the work of Tibor Vágó, unveiled in 1996.*

Equestrian statue of Francis II Rákóczi. *The work of János Pásztor from 1937, it portrays the elected prince of Transylvania and commander of the Hungarian insurgent forces, who defended the country against the Habsburgs during the period 1703 to 1711.*

Ethnographic Museum. *Designed by Alajos Hauszmann, the former Palace of the Supreme Royal Court was built in Neo-Renaissance style between 1893 and 1896. A team of three horses draw the carriage of the goddess of Justice at the peak of the tympanum of the building's delicately proportioned main front. The monumental ceiling fresco painted by Károly Lotz depicts the triumph of Justitia. Today, the building houses the national ethnographic collections.*

CHAIN BRIDGE

Count István Széchenyi, a distinguished figure of the Hungarian reform period, did not spare efforts in order to achieve one of his most ambitious dreams, building a permanent bridge to connect the two cities. After founding the Bridge Society in 1832, he made a trip to England where he observed the first chain bridge in Marlow, designed by the English engineer William T. Clark. As a result of the visit, Clark was commissioned to design a bridge in Hungary. Construction began in 1839 under the supervision of Adam Clark (no relation). The work lasted for 10 years. Despite the war of independence, the siege of Buda and the attempts of the Austrian army to explode it, the bridge was opened on November 20th 1849.

The Chain Bridge is a 380-metre long, 15.7-metre wide suspension bridge. The ends of the chains, laced through the triumphal arch-shaped portals over the two piers, were secured inside underground chambers on the two riverbanks. The stone lions guarding the abutments are the works of János Marschalkó (1852). Blown up in January 1945 by the retreating German army, the rebuilding of the bridge in its original form was completed in 1949. Traffic along the Chain Bridge between central Pest and Buda passes through the Buda Tunnel. The 350-metre long Tunnel, designed by Adam Clark, was built from 1853 to 1857.

View with Buda Palace. Heavily decorated cast-iron chandeliers have been aligned along the bridge.

View of Pest from the Castle Hill. The Chain Bridge was the first permanent bridge to connect Buda and Pest and the western and eastern regions of the country.

The row of Pest hotels and the riverside promenade with pleasure-boats and restaurant boats. This is where the first international hotel was opened after WWII, in 1970.

HUNGARIAN ACADEMY OF SCIENCES

The Neo-Renaissance palace, built from 1862 to 1865, was designed by Berlin architect Friedrich A. Stüler and Miklós Ybl. The construction was financed from public donations. The street front is decorated with the allegoric statues of various branches of science. The statues on the corners were modelled on distinguished academics. The frescoes of the Eclectic banquet hall, symbolizing science and the arts are the works of Károly Lotz. The statue of István Széchenyi, 'the greatest Hungarian', outside the palace is by József Engel.

The bronze relief shows the moment the Academy was founded by István Széchenyi by offering one year's income for its construction.

Statue of Ferenc Deák. The work of Adolf Huszár (1887), the statue is surrounded by several hundred-year old trees on Roosevelt Square. The sitting figure, 'the wise man of Hungary', served as a minister in the first Hungarian government accountable to Parliament, and later played a major role in preparing the 1867 Compromise with Austria.

Peacock gate. *The gate's fine contours make the monumental wrought-iron gate a Secessionist masterpiece.*

GRESHAM PALACE

Gresham was the name of a London-based insurance company, which commissioned the building for its headquarters. Prominent even from remote points on the other side of the Danube, the palace is located at the classiest spot of the Pest riverfront, in the axis of the Chain Bridge. Its ornate façade, reliefs, tiny mosaics and a mass of gables and pinnacles have made it one of the finest examples of Art Nouveau architecture in Budapest. Splendidly restored recently, the building has been turned into a luxury hotel.

The Lounge. *During the two world wars, the fashionable Gresham coffee-house was a meeting-point for progressive intellectuals.*

SAINT STEPHEN'S CATHEDRAL

In 1845, József Hild was commissioned to design the largest church of the capital. After his death in 1867, Miklós Ybl took over supervision of the construction, making subtle alterations in Italian Neo-Renaissance style to Hild's original Neoclassical design. After fifty years of construction, the building was completed by József Kauser. The external view of the building reflects its pure internal layout. The twin-steeple, broad, open main front with a staircase facing the Danube offers a splendid view from the square, impressively covered with colourful marble mosaic, a more recent addition. The main entrance is shaped like a triumphal arch. A pair of Corinthian responds support the tympanum whose relief portrays the Hungarian saints pay homage to the Virgin Mary, guardian of Hungary. The mosaic between the columns depicts King St. Stephen and the resurrection of Christ. The Cathedral was consecrated in 1905.

The dome, *65 metres high, has a diameter of 22 metres. The mosaic shows the Holy Father surrounded by the figures of Jesus, the angels and the prophets. The four evangelists are depicted in the arched triangles under the dome.*

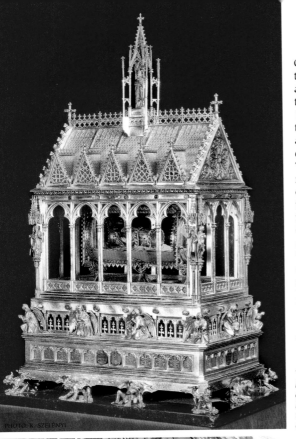

PHOTO: K. SZELÉNYI

Its ground-plan shaped like a Greek cross, the Cathedral is the finest example of Eclectic architecture in Hungary. It has impressive dimensions at a length of 86 metres and a width of 55 metres. Burnt down during WWII and rebuilt in 1948-1949, its 96-metre high dome is the highest church tower in Budapest. The interior of the Cathedral and the sanctuary are decorated with the works of important Hungarian artists (Károly Lotz, Mór Than, Gyula Benczúr, Bertalan Székely, Árpád Feszty, Alajos Stróbl and Pál Pátzay). The right tower commands an exceptional view of the city. It holds the country's largest bell, weighing 9 tons, a gift from the readers of the 'Neue Bildpost' German Christian weekly in order to replace the old bell, requisitioned by the German army in 1944. During WWII, the most important documents of the Archives were deposited in the extensive crypt, considered bomb-proof, of the Cathedral, along with lots of valuable works of art and historical objects. In 2004, it became the cathedral of the Esztergom-Budapest diocese, equal in rank with the Esztergom Main Cathedral.

The Holy Right. *The left aisle opens to the Chapel of the Holy Right. It is here that the right hand of Saint Stephen of Hungary, preserved intact in a mummified state, is kept as a relic in a preciously decorated reliquary. This is the starting point of the Saint Stephen's Day procession on August 20th each year.*

The back elevation. The semicircular sanctuary at the back-front, of classically noble proportions emphasised with a peristyle of Ionic columns, was designed by Miklós Ybl. Statues of the four evangelists have been placed in the outside niches of the dome while those of the twelve apostles, the work of Leó Feszler, are lined up along the border crowning the vestry.

Altar of the Virgin Mary. The gem of the altar at the southern end of the transept was painted by Gyula Benczúr. The altarpiece depicts St. Stephen offering the crown that represents his country to the Virgin.

The high altar with the life-size Carrara marble statue of St. Stephen. The work of Alajos Stróbl, St. Stephen's statue stands in the apse of the sanctuary. The bronze reliefs in the background show scenes from the life of the first king of Hungary. The patches of the semidome above the sanctuary have been covered with mosaics by Gyula Benczúr, allegorically picturing the five parts of the mass.

The Tympanum.

GO SUM VIA VERITAS ET VITA

ELISABETH BRIDGE

Designed by Aurél Czekelius, the Elisabeth Bridge was built at the narrowest point of the Danube between 1897 and 1903. Spanning a distance of 290 metres, it held the record of the longest suspension bridge until 1926. All seven bridges including the Erzsébet Bridge were blown up by the retreating German army in the siege of Budapest in 1945. Its fate became uncertain until the construction, 1961 to 1964, of the elegant new cable bridge designed by Pál Sávoly. Salvaged pieces of the structural elements of the former bridge are kept at the Museum of Transport and the University of Engineering.

The Gellért Hill rises abruptly to a height of 235 metres above the city at the Buda abutment of Erzsébet Bridge. Up until the late 19th century, these were the outskirts of Buda. A former wine-growing neighbourhood, the area between the Gellért Hill and the Danube is called the Tabán. Legend has it that King Matthias himself used to frequent the Rác Baths located at the southern tip of the Tabán park.

The Belvárosi (Inner City) parish church at the Pest abutment is Pest's oldest building. According to legend, St. Elisabeth of Hungary was betrothed to Ludwig IV of Thuringia in this church.

Rudas baths. *Several medicinal baths were erected over the hot springs at the bottom of the Gellért Hill. It was here that the Turkish Pasha Sokoli Mustapha built the largest of the Turkish baths after 1566. Twenty-one hot springs gush forth from under the hill, in close*

Queen Elisabeth's statue. *The statue was reinstated in 1986 in the park north of the Buda abutment. A classy work by György Zala (1932), who laid particular emphasis on the female beauty of the Hungarophile queen (1837-1898).*

St. Gellért's monument. *Legend has it that the missionary Gellért, bishop of Csanád, was hurled off the mountain by a group of Hungarians in an act of religious defiance in 1064. The statue of the bishop was erected in 1904 in the backdrop of a semicircular colonnade cut into the hillside. With the waterfall below, evening floodlight gives the monument a captivating effect.*

proximity. The baths are centred around the domed hall, 10 metres in diameter, with an octagonal pool, surrounded by a wagon-roofed passage. The baths, recently renovated to high standards, are popular with locals and tourists alike.

38

LIBERTY BRIDGE

The Liberty Bridge was built in order to connect the Fővám and Gellért Squares according to designs by János Feketeházy during 1894-1896. Originally christened Franz Joseph Bridge, it was the emperor himself who hammered the first silver rivet into the steel structure on the Pest side. Mythical turul birds and highly ornamented Hungarian coats-of-arms decorate the turret-like protrusions and gates emphasising the latticed structure. Blown up by the Germans, the rebuilding was completed in 1946.

Central Market-Hall. Having a ground plan that has proved practical to this day, the market-hall was designed by Samu Petz, while its steel structures were produced by Gustav Eiffel (1892-96). The outside front is covered with coloured bricks framed by Neo-Gothic stonework. A corner turret covered with patterned majolica stands on each side of the main gate. The exceptionally wide range of fresh food on offer means that the market-hall always teems with customers.

Cave church on the Gellért Hill. Modelled on the cave of Lourdes, the church was built inside a natural cave in 1926. In 1951, the church was destroyed and its entrance walled up overnight. It was returned into the custody of the Order of St. Paul in 1989.

The Liberty Bridge with the Gellért Hill and the Citadel. The magnificent contours of the bridge were dreamt up by Virgil Nagy.

GELLÉRT BATHS

The peculiar domed mass of the Gellért Hotel and Thermal Baths dominates the Art Nouveau atmosphere of St. Gellért Square. A Johannite hospital used to operate here from the 12th century. The Gellért is the largest of the baths erected over the string of medicinal springs of the Buda side of the river. In the Turkish period, people not only bathed in the muddy open-air Achik Illidze bath, but also carried its water home. While the miraculous mud has run out by now, you can still enjoy the curative effects of the water. The wonderful Secessionist buildings of the baths and the hotel were built in 1918, whereas the effervescent pool and the pool with artificial waves were completed in 1927. The various rooms of the baths surround the central domed hall reminiscent of the layout of classic Roman public baths. Open-

air terraces and pools were added at the back of the building, facing the hill. The hotel is located in the front, facing the square.

The water of over ten springs flows from underground into the extravagantly furnished baths at the average temperature of 46 °C. These springs supply the effervescent pool, the indoor pump-room, the bubble and tub baths, the steam baths and, in the summer, the pool with artificial waves. Their excellent water contains calcium, magnesium, hydrocarbonate, sulphate and fluoride, used effectively in the treatment of articular and spinal diseases and cardiovascular troubles.

Sunset view *of the Gellért Hotel, whose international reputation rests partly on its magnificent Art Nouveau splendour.*

The imposing street front of the Gellért Hotel. Mineral water flows from the drinking fountain in front of the hotel. In the sixties, the lounge was converted in a kind of conservative modernist style typical of the time.

The Secessionist pool hall. The walls are lavishly decorated with Zsolnay tiles of magnificent colours.

Pool with artificial waves. Surrounded by terraces and a pleasant park, the pool equipped with a wave-generator is located behind the building complex of the baths and the hotel.

The effervescent pool. The pool can be accessed through the mosaic-floored entrance hall on the right. The 30-metre long effervescent pool and a thermal pool of the temperature of 36 °C have been located inside the hall having a convertible roof.

The riverside Promenade. *The hundred-year-old Promenade commands a magnificent vista on the Danube.*

INNER CITY – THE PEST VIGADÓ

Designed by Frigyes Feszl, the Pest Vigadó was built during 1859-1864 as a luxury venue for celebrations, concerts and balls. With its highly articulated, symmetric façade, the building is a most sublime example of Romantic architecture. Above the single-story archway, the wall-faces, imitating mysterious lace trimmings, are decorated with battlemented, turreted columns and enormous semicircular windows. Its lavishly gilded, huge entrance hall and banquet hall of enchanting beauty are adorned with frescoes by Mór Than and Károly Lotz. It has been a venue for high-quality concerts and celebrations since its opening in 1865.

Princess statuette. *The elfin Princess, completed by László Marton in 1989, is perched on the hand-rail at the tram stop outside the Vigadó.*

Gerbeaud pastry-shop on Vörösmarty Square. *Named after the distinguished confectioner Emil Gerbeaud of Genevan origin, the shop soon earned international fame on account of its exquisite furnishing and extraordinary range of cakes.*

Statue of Mihály Vörösmarty.
Erected at the centre of the square, the Carrara marble statue is a monument to a great poet of the Hungarian nation.

VÁCI STREET

The famous shopping and pedestrian street stretches between Vörösmarty Square and the Market-Hall, past the Elisabeth Bridge. That was about the entire length of Pest during the Middle Ages. With fashion-shops and gift-stores, it was already an important main street in the 18th century. 'The smallest street of Pest is a real treasure-house of gems and jewellery', raved a contemporary.

The twin towers of the Klotild Palace stand as gateposts at the abutment on the Pest side of Elisabeth Bridge. The palaces, built in 1902 in Neo-Baroque, late Eclectic style, were named after the customer, wife of the Archduke Joseph.

With a history of nearly two thousand years, the Bel-városi (Inner City) parish church has preserved various bits of all these centuries. Before the church was built, a watch-tower had stood here, surrounded by the ever-expanding city of Pest.

Hermes Fountain. The fountain, work of an unknown sculptor, was set up in Váci Street in 1983. It portrays Hermes, the tricky thievish God, messenger of the Greek gods and attendant of the dead souls, with the caducean staff.

Thonet Building, 11 Váci Street. Designed by Secessionist architect Ödön Lechner, the house is decked with highly adorned Zsolnay pyrogranite tiles and a wrought-iron balustrade (1890).

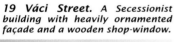

19 Váci Street. A Secessionist building with heavily ornamented façade and a wooden shop-window.

Great Synagogue. *Designed by Ludwig Förster, the Synagogue was built 1854 to 1859 in Romantic, Byzantine/Moorish style. It is Europe's largest active synagogue. Between its gilded onion-shaped towers, the rosewindow engrossed in the wall is covered with stripes of coloured ceramic tiles.*

The Danubius Fountain on Erzsébet Square. *The figure at the top represents the Danube, while the ones below are symbols of the three main tributaries (Tisza, Drava & Sava) (1883).*

The Hungarian National Museum. *Designed by Mihály Pollack, the museum was built between 1837 and 1846 in the Neoclassical style. The group of statues on the tympanum is the work of Raffaello Monti. A symbol of historical Pannonia, the seated female figure in the middle is offering a pair of laurel wreaths with both hands to the figures impersonating Science and the Arts on her right and Fame and History on her left. The foundations of Hungary's greatest museum were laid by Ferenc Széchenyi by bestowing his entire library, art and numismatic collections onto the nation in 1802. Since the rally of March 15th 1848, the building has become a symbol of the revolution. Today, it houses the Museums of National History and Natural History.*

Nyugati (Western) Railway Station. *The building, designed by August de Serres, was constructed by the Paris-based Eiffel Company during 1874-1877. In keeping with contemporary tastes, both side annexes were crowned with a pair of turreted roof sections in the French style. The steel structure has a lateral span of 40 metres and a height of 26 metres.*

New York Palace. *Erzsébet körút (Boulevard). Designed by Alajos Hauszmann, it was built between 1891 and 1895 in Neo-Renaissance/Eclectic style as the headquarters of a US-based insurance company. The fashionable café operating on the ground-floor at the time has a special place in Hungarian literary history. The building is now utilised as a hotel.*

Vígszínház. *At the time it was first opened in 1896, the theatre was located almost on the outskirts of the city. The domed Neo-Baroque/Eclectic building was designed by the Vienna-based Fellner & Helmer company. The bronze busts of the poets Miklós Zrínyi and Sándor Petőfi are found outside the arched façade. The busts of famous actors and actresses are lined up in the foyer and the passages. Today, it is one of the most popular theatres in Budapest.*

The sanctuary lamp of Lajos Batthyány. *It was here that Count Lajos Batthyány, Prime Minister of the first Hungarian government accountable to Parliament was executed by the Austrians on October 6th 1849. The light in the glass cage of the bronze lantern erected in his memory has not gone out since 1926.*

The New National Theatre. *The latest addition to Budapest's theatres, located in the immediate neighbourhood of the Lágymányosi Bridge, the National Theatre was designed by Mária Siklós. It was opened for the public in 2002.*

MUSEUM OF APPLIED ARTS

Designed by Ödön Lechner and Gyula Pártos, the Museum was built between 1893 and 1896. Having made a bold break with the traditional historical, eclectic style of Hungarian architecture, Lechner introduced a Secessionist style with a typical Hungarian flavour. No wonder that his oeuvre has been likened to that of Gaudi by a distinguished British historian of architecture. In addition to the Hungarian folk motifs, he also used elements of Oriental decoration on the walls lavishly covered with coloured Zsolnay pyrogranite and majolica. The ceiling and side walls of the main entrance hall are covered with richly coloured Zsolnay majolica inspired by Sassanian and Iranian motifs. The tiles covering the high octagonal dome are glazed green and yellow.

Nearly a hundred thousand objects are kept in the museum's collections, including important furniture, textile, gold and silversmith, ceramics, book-binding and glasswork collections.

The Museum interior. The first impression in the vestibule is awe-inspiring. There is unobstructed view through the open ceiling up to the stained-glass windows covering the hall. Highly ornamented stairways lead upstairs. On both sides, galleries have been attached to the main hall whose Oriental-looking foiled arches are ornamented with stuck moulding. The light penetrating the arched glass ceiling produces a liberating, ethereal feel. This special atmosphere makes it a suitable venue for high-profile receptions and meetings.

Post-Office Savings Bank building. 4 Hold Street. Designed by Ödön Lechner, this splendid Art Nouveau building completed in 1900 bears the unique touch of his creator. While the structure is simple, its façade is heavily adorned. The arched battlement between the raw brick pillars is decked with flower mosaics strongly rooted in Hungarian folk art. The ridges, turrets and chimneys covered with glazed Zsolnay majolica make a compelling sight. The marble staircase and the pay-office also boast a unique design. Today, it is the building of the National Bank.

Török Bank Building. 3 Szervita Square. 'The Glorification of Hungary' is depicted in the glass mosaic set in the frontispiece of the pure glass façade of this Secessionist building (1906).

Liszt Ferenc Music Academy. 8 Liszt Ferenc Square. The foyer of the Academy is adorned with a magnificent Art Nouveau fresco by Aladár Körösfői-Kriesch. It is entitled 'Whoever seeketh life, must make a pilgrimage to the sources of Art'.

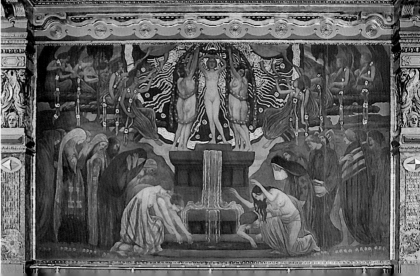

THE OPERA

A long-awaited moment in the history of Hungarian opera came on September 27th 1884, when the Budapest Opera House was first opened to the public by a magnificent celebration attended by Franz Joseph I. Ferenc Erkel's Bánk Bán and Wagner's Lohengrin were also performed at the command performance. At the time, it was the most modern opera house in Europe, with practical and artistic considerations brought into harmony in its design.

Designed by Miklós Ybl, the greatest Hungarian architect who played a crucial role in the shaping of the face of Budapest, and built 1875 to 1884, the Neo-Renaissance building of the Opera is a harmonious mix of Renaissance and Baroque stylistic elements, architecture, plastic art and ornamentation. Even the smallest details (chandeliers, lamp-brackets and door-handles) were designed by the architect himself. The sheer diversity of the series of exterior and interior spaces makes for an entrancing sight.

Most of the frescoes in the building are by the three greatest masters of Hungarian historicism, Károly Lotz, Bertalan Székely and Mór Than. The fresco cycles, modelled on Parisian examples, are expressions of the universality and apotheosis of music.

During the over one hundred years of its existence, the Opera has earned worldwide reputation on account of its directors, excellent singers, ballet and orchestra.

Main façade. The statues of four of the Greek Muses (Terpsichore, Erato, Thalia and Melpomene) stand in the corner niches of the building's façade. The balustrade of the crown moulding carries the figures of 16 best-known opera composers (Mozart, Beethoven, Rossini, Verdi, Bizet, Tchaikovsky, etc.). The main entrance is decorated with Carrara marble sphinxes and magnificent iron candelabra.

Statue of Franz Liszt. The statues at the sides of the main entrance are the works of Zsigmond Kisfaludy Stróbl. The statue to the left shows composer Ferenc Erkel, the first chief musical director of the Budapest Opera.

The auditorium. The horse-shoe shaped auditorium is enclosed by three stories of rows of boxes. The box of honour is adorned with statues symbolising the four main timbres. The ceiling is partly covered by a huge fresco entitled 'Mount Olympus and the Gods' by Károly Lotz. The gold and copper radiance of the theatre is heightened by the over 6,600 lb bronze chandelier, made in Mainz, Germany.

Staircase. The marble staircase, the most ambitious interior space designed by Miklós Ybl, emphasises the representative function of the building. The ceiling is decorated with frescoes by Mór Than.

The Royal Staircase leads directly to the royal box from the arcaded driveway of the building.

HEROES' SQUARE

The Millennium Monument dominating Heroes' Square was built for the millennium of the Magyar conquest and the existence of Hungary. The construction began in 1896 but was not completed until 1929. The total length of the two parts of the semicircular colonnade is 85 metres. It was designed, along with the 36-metre high pillar at the centre, by architect Albert Schickedanz and sculptor György Zala. The bronze figure protectively spreading his wings at the top of the pillar is the archangel Gabriel, a traditional symbol of triumph. The work of György Zala, it earned a grand prize at the 1900 World's Fair in Paris. The pedestal carries the equestrian statues of the seven conquering chiefs, with Prince Árpád in the middle. A Pantheon of Hungarian history, the statues of Hungarian kings, princes and commanders have been positioned between the columns of the arched colonnade, altogether seven distinguished personalities on both sides. The reliefs below each bronze statue depict historical scenes from the lives of the respective hero.

During WWII, the decorative pavement was destroyed. It was restored in 1980 with a pavement in keeping with the 1938 design. For over a hundred years, the square has been the venue of major celebrations, rallies and demonstrations, including the International Eucharistic Congress, 1938, the re-burial of Imre Nagy and his companions martyred in the 1956 revolution, 1989, and the holy mass celebrated by John Paul II in 1991.

Andrássy Street. *The 2.5 km-long avenue, bordered with decorative mansions, runs into Heroes' Square.*

The chariot of War is depicted running at full speed in the interior nook of the left-side colonnade.

The archangel Gabriel holding the Holy Crown and the double cross.

The chariot of Peace stands on the right-side interior butt pier.

Famous Hungarian kings. The Hungarian kings St. Ladislaus, Louis I and Matthias. Below each statue, there is a relief recalling a significant moment in the lives of the monarchs.

Heroes' Monument. The monument of the soldiers fallen in the world wars has been set up in front of the statues of the chiefs. Hungarian and foreign statesmen pay respect to them on national holidays.

Equestrian statues of Prince Árpád and the conquering chiefs. The sheer scale and detail of this group of equestrian statues by György Zala make it a unique work of art.

Museum of Fine Arts. The Museum, designed by Albert Schickedanz and Fülöp Herzog in Eclectic/Neoclassical style, was opened to the public in 1906. The last great example of Hungarian Eclectic architecture, its main front was divided into several parts, while its Corinthian colonnade is closed with triple tympanums. The central relief is a faithful copy of the western sculptural group of the Zeus temple on Mount Olympus. It shows a scene from the battle of the Centaurs and the Lapiths. Inside, a two-storey-high roofed court with huge loggias is surrounded by stately halls designed in a Renaissance spirit.

Donations by aristocrats, Church dignitaries and rich citizens laid the foundations of the internationally renowned collection of the Museum. The various collections include antique, Egyptian, Greek and Roman, medieval and modern paintings and sculptures. Temporary exhibitions of the works of celebrated artists are also held on a regular basis.

THE GALLERY OF ART

Designed by Albert Schickedanz and Fülöp Herzog in Eclectic/Neoclassical style, Hungary's biggest art exhibition venue was completed in 1895. The mosaic by Jenő Haranghy in the ridge of the façade is entitled St. Stephen, a patron of the arts. The building is covered all over with varied and high-coloured ceramic ornamentation. Throughout the past century, the evenly lit, spacious exhibition rooms behind the artistic façade have proved a suitable home for the cream of contemporary Hungarian art. Temporary international exhibitions are also held in the Gallery.

The brick-covered building is lavishly decorated with splendid Zsolnay ceramic tiles.

THE CITY PARK

Budapest's largest park, located north of Heroes' Square, covers an area of one square kilometre. Parliaments and fairs used to be held here in the days of old. Bestowed upon the City by Leopold I, it was planted mainly with sycamore maples and horse-chestnut trees. It became the first European public park in municipal custody. The park was popular with people of all social classes, aristocrats on horseback or taking a coach ride, commoners on foot. The most important event in its history was the Millennium Exhibition opened on May 2nd 1896. In summer, the pond is a popular destination for a romantic boat ride, while in the winter it functions as a skating rink. Scattered around the City Park, there are lots of interesting statues as well as the mock medieval Vajdahunyad Castle, the museums of transport and of agriculture, the Zoological and Botanical Gardens, the Circus, the Amusement Park and the Széchenyi Baths.

The Elephant House. *This Oriental/Secessionist building was designed by Károly Kós.*

Zoological and Botanical Gardens: the Art Nouveau main entrance. *The internationally renowned Zoological Gardens were opened in 1866 over an area of 16 hectares. Over 500 animal species are kept here in an environment similar to their natural habitats.*

The Museum of Transport *showcases all types of transport. The Museum boasts unrivalled railway model and navigation collections.*

VAJDAHUNYAD CASTLE

Historical Building Complex by its official name, the castle, made up of 21 parts, was designed by Ignác Alpár for the 1896 Millennium Exhibition. According to the competition rules, the group of buildings had to represent all architectural styles of Hungary, while giving a homogeneous impression. Originally built with a temporary frame structure, the castle became so popular it was converted during 1904 to 1908 with more lasting building materials into its present-day form. The building complex is divided into Romanesque, Gothic, Renaissance and Baroque sections.

A stone-bridge leads to the massive Gothic main gate on Széchenyi Island. The towers and chapels in the courtyard are faithful copies of historical buildings from all around the country. Right of the main gate, the tower and the four-pillared hall of the eponymous Vajdahunyad Castle of Transylvania constitute the most remarkable part of the castle.

One of the palaces of the representative mass of the Baroque buildings accommodates the Museum of Agriculture.

The Tower of Torture. *The tower rising on the left of the main gate was designed in imitation of the typical bastion style of castles in northern Hungary.*

Statue of Anonymus. *The work of Miklós Liget (1903) portrays the anonymous chronicler of King Béla III. An apt artistic idea befitting the mysterious chronicler, his features are hid behind a large hood.*

The Archer's Statue. *The work of Zsigmond Kisfaludi Stróbl, the statue was completed in 1929.*

The Ják Chapel. *An imitation of the main gate, decorated with the figures of the apostles, of the Romanesque Abbey of the Transdanubian village of Ják. On the left, there is a Romanesque cloister court with an ambulatory.*

SZÉCHENYI BATHS

Thermal springs abound in Budapest as in few other metropolises. First opened in 1913, the Széchenyi Baths in the scenic City Park are one of Europe's biggest and hottest spas, open all year round. Designed by Győző Czigler and Ede Dvorzsák, it was built between 1909 and 1903 in Eclectic style. Its four smaller domes on the four corners encircle a higher and more heavily adorned one in the centre. The building was enlarged in 1927 with the addition of three large open-air pools. Services include steam baths and hot tubs, saunas and a fitness room with massage.

Pools with medicinal water. *The first artesian spring was explored here in 1877. It still supplies the pools along with mineral waters from later explorations. Gushing from depths of 1,000 to 1,300 metres, the water reaches the surface at about 70-80 °C. Besides other curative effects, it provides an effective treatment for arthritis.*

The dome over the main entrance. *The domed hall of the main entrance is decorated with Art Nouveau glass mosaics by Miksa Róth, including the Chariot of the Sun high up inside the dome.*

Terraces. *The terraces have been divided into separate female and male sunbathing sections.*

Aquincum. *Explorations of the ruins of the Roman city began in 1880. The dwelling-houses in the city surrounded by a wall reinforced with battlements were fitted with an aqueduct, sewers, some with floor heating.*

Women carrying umbrellas. *Óbuda. Located at the northern side of the main square, this sculptural group is the work of Imre Varga.*

Corvin Square. *Built on medieval foundations, these ancient houses are adorned with Baroque stone balconies and reliefs. The bronze figure on the ornamental fountain by Lajos Millacher is a Hungarian knight with a drinking horn.*

Pest-side view of the Víziváros. The Calvinist church building (1893-96) on Szilágyi Dezső Square rises above the skyline of the Buda riverside. The statue of the designer, Samu Petz stands behind the Neo-Gothic church covered with Zsolnay tiles. The bulk of the Matthias Church and the Fisherman's bastion looms in the background.

Church of St. Anna. This Baroque Catholic church on Batthyány Square was built from 1740 to 1762. The statues of eponymous St. Anna and the child Mary were positioned on the lavishly decorated main front. The interior of the church is also remarkable.

Margaret Island. This 80-hectare island is an enormous park with pathways, hotels and thermal baths.

Király baths. 82-86 Fő Street. One of the most important historic buildings from the Turkish period, the baths was built between 1566 and 1570. The dome in the centre of the Turkish part of the building rises over an octagonal pool with several stairways. The main hall is surrounded by various smaller arched rooms. Its hot mineral waters are used for the treatment of locomotion diseases.

BUDAPEST

1 - Houses of
   Parliament

2 - Chain Bridge

3 - Elisabeth Bridge

4 - Citadel

5 - Buda Castle

6 - Fisherman's Bastion,
   Matthias Church

7 - Saint Stephen's
   Cathedral

8 - Opera

9 - Nyugati (Western)
   Railway Station

10 - Heroes' Square,
   Gallery of Art

11 - City Park,
   Vajdahunyad Castle

12 - Széchenyi Baths

13 - Great Synagogue

14 - Hungarian
   National Museum

15 - Central Market-Hall

16 - Liberty Bridge

17 - Gellért Baths

18 - National Theatre

19 - Margaret Island

ISBN 978-963-87573-1-9

© Private edition
Huber Pál Kolozs
Phone: 00-36-302 536 342

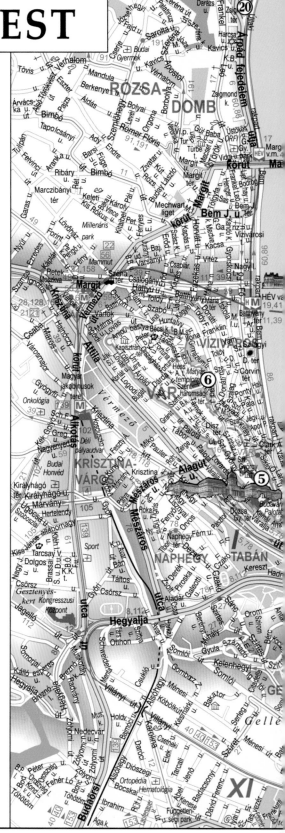